God Is Listening When You Pray

Children's Christian Prayer Books

Speedy Publishing LLC
40 E. Main St. #1156
Newark, DE 19711
www.speedypublishing.com

Reciting a prayer is like introducing them to the wisdom of God.

It is important to teach our children how to pray.

God hears our every prayer. Prayer is just like talking to our mom and dad, except we're talking to our Heavenly Father.

TRACE THE SENTENCES.

Prayer for Everyday

Dear Father in Heaven

Watch over me as I begin

the day for your glory

Thank you for giving me

this brand new day

A day to behold and to cherish

To enjoy the life , to be

kind to others

To love my family and to

love Jesus Your Son.

Amen

REWRITE THE SENTENCES.

TRACE THE SENTENCES.

Prayer for Everyday

Dear Father in Heaven
Watch over me as I begin
the day for your glory
Thank you for giving me
this brand new day
A day to behold and to cherish
To enjoy the life , to be kind to others
To love my family and to
love Jesus Your Son.
Amen

REWRITE THE SENTENCES.

TRACE THE SENTENCES.

Thank You Jesus

Jesus, I love you.
Thank you for making me your friend
Thank you for not leaving me

Thank you for being a brother
Your love makes me dance in glee

Thank you for the inspiration
To live and to love.
Amen

REWRITE THE SENTENCES.

TRACE THE SENTENCES.

Thank You Jesus

Jesus, I love you.
Thank you for making me your friend
Thank you for not leaving me

Thank you for being a brother
Your love makes me dance in glee

Thank you for the inspiration
To live and to love.
Amen

REWRITE THE SENTENCES.

TRACE THE SENTENCES.

The Powerful God

Heavenly Father,

You created a beautiful world

I feel your greatness in the

beautiful flowers that I see

In the blue skies and ten cottony clouds

I feel your warmth in the shining sun

You give me freedom

to enjoy them all

Like the birds flying in the skies

As I have my mom and dad

All is set, all is free

Perfectly made for everybody!

REWRITE THE SENTENCES.

TRACE THE SENTENCES.

The Powerful God

Heavenly Father,

You created a beautiful world

I feel your greatness in the

beautiful flowers that I see

In the blue skies and ten cottony clouds

I feel your warmth in the shining sun

You give me freedom to enjoy them all

Like the birds flying in the skies

As I have my mom and dad

All is set, all is free

Perfectly made for everybody!

REWRITE THE SENTENCES.

TRACE THE SENTENCES.

Jesus is Everybody's Friend

Jesus I feel your great
love for all of us
You never leave us nor forsake us
You are a true friend
I can feel your presence
Every time I gaze at the blue seas
I can feel your love
Every time I see my friends
I know you hear me when I say
I love you more and more.
Amen

REWRITE THE SENTENCES.

TRACE THE SENTENCES.

Jesus is Everybody's Friend

Jesus I feel your great love for all of us

You never leave us nor forsake us

You are a true friend

I can feel your presence

Every time I gaze at the blue seas

I can feel your love

Every time I see my friends

I know you hear me when I say

I love you more and more.

Amen

REWRITE THE SENTENCES.

TRACE THE SENTENCES.

Prayer for Peace

Lord, Our Father

You are the source of great

wisdom and compassion

Of love and of unity

Grant us peace

And set the world with your love

Make us love another as we love you

Make us like brothers and sisters

Just like Jesus, our brother

Keep us united in your love.

Amen

REWRITE THE SENTENCES.

TRACE THE SENTENCES.

Prayer for Peace

Lord, Our Father

You are the source of great

wisdom and compassion

Of love and of unity

Grant us peace

And set the world with your love

Make us love another as we love you

Make us like brothers and sisters

Just like Jesus, our brother

Keep us united in your love.

Amen

REWRITE THE SENTENCES.

TRACE THE SENTENCES.

Prayer for a Clean Heart

Thank you Lord for giving me life
A life I treasure
Thank you for giving me a heart
Keep it always clean and pure
Make me love others so dearly
Like the way you love me
Grant me pure thoughts
That will guide me
To be kind to others
And to be truthful in your love.
Amen

REWRITE THE SENTENCES.

TRACE THE SENTENCES.

Prayer for a Clean Heart

Thank you Lord for giving me life

A life I treasure

Thank you for giving me a heart

Keep it always clean and pure

Make me love others so dearly

Like the way you love me

Grant me pure thoughts

That will guide me

To be kind to others

And to be truthful in your love.

Amen

REWRITE THE SENTENCES.

TRACE THE SENTENCES.

Prayer for Great Happiness

Lord, you are the source
of love and wisdom
Your son Jesus is the source
of love and mercy
Grant us great happiness
By sharing the blessings we receive
By loving others unconditionally
By living with your great compassion.
Amen

REWRITE THE SENTENCES.

TRACE THE SENTENCES.

Prayer for Great Happiness

Lord, you are the source
of love and wisdom
Your son Jesus is the source
of love and mercy
Grant us great happiness
By sharing the blessings we receive
By loving others unconditionally
By living with your great compassion.
Amen

REWRITE THE SENTENCES.

TRACE THE SENTENCES.

Prayer for Great Happiness

Lord, you are the source
of love and wisdom
Your son Jesus is the source
of love and mercy
Grant us great happiness
By sharing the blessings we receive
By loving others unconditionally
By living with your great compassion.
Amen

REWRITE THE SENTENCES.

TRACE THE SENTENCES.

Prayer for Great Happiness

Lord, you are the source
of love and wisdom
Your son Jesus is the source
of love and mercy
Grant us great happiness
By sharing the blessings we receive
By loving others unconditionally
By living with your great compassion.
Amen

REWRITE THE SENTENCES.

Visit
BABY PROFESSOR
EDUCATION KIDS
www.BabyProfessorBooks.com
to download Free Baby Professor eBooks
and view our catalog of new and exciting
Children's Books

www.ingramcontent.com/pod-product-compliance
Lightning Source LLC
LaVergne TN
LVHW060627170826
845677LV00027B/1716
* 9 7 9 8 8 6 9 4 4 4 8 7 5 *